The Nature of Yearning

The Nature of Yearning
POEMS BY DAVID HUDDLE

PEREGRINE SMITH BOOKS
SALT LAKE CITY

First edition
96 95 94 93 92   5 4 3 2 1

Copyright © 1992 by David Huddle

All rights reserved. No portion of this book may be reproduced in any manner whatsoever without written permission from the publisher.

Published by Gibbs Smith, Publisher, Peregrine Smith Books
P.O. Box 667, Layton, Utah 84041 (801) 544-9800

Design by Kathleen Timmerman

On the cover:
Albert Bierstadt, American (1830-1902)
Mountain Brook, the White Mountains, New Hampshire (1863), oil on board, Duke University Museum of Art Purchase, Elizabeth Von Canon Fund

Photograph of David Huddle by Marion Ettlinger

Printed and bound in the United States of America

Library of Congress Cataloging-in-Publication Data

Huddle, David.
    The nature of yearning / David Huddle.
        p. cm.—(the Peregrine Smith poetry series)
    ISBN 0-87905-459-X : $9.95
    I. Title. II. Series.
PS3558.U287N38 1992
811'.54—dc20   91-40721
                                                        CIP

for Lindsey, Bess, and Molly

OTHER BOOKS BY DAVID HUDDLE

FICTION:
  A Dream With No Stump Roots In it
  Only the Little Bone
  The High Spirits
  Intimates

POETRY:
  Paper Boy
  Stopping by Home

ESSAYS:
  The Writing Habit

Table of Contents

1	LOCAL METAPHYSICS
3	EASTERN STANDARD
4	STUDY
5	THE NATURE OF YEARNING
10	VISIT OF THE HAWK
11	INSIDE THE HUMMINGBIRD AVIARY
12	PERSPECTIVE
13	THE FEEDER
14	FEEDER IN THE DARK
15	THE SNOW MONKEY ARGUES WITH GOD
16	DISCOVERY CHANNEL
17	PARTY POEM
19	AMERICAN HISTORY
20	THE SWIMMER
23	THE QUICK
24	QUIET HOUR
26	MUSIC
27	THE BIRDS
28	SUMMER LAKE
31	ASYLUM
33	CREATION MYTH
35	A FIELD IN NORTH DAKOTA
38	THE DANCE
39	LOVE AND ART
40	UPSTAIRS HALLWAY, 5 A.M.
41	CLOSE
42	ANOTHER FATHER'S STORY
44	CATCH
45	THINKING ABOUT MY FATHERS

Local Metaphysics

Finally the mother had to pack up the kids
in the car and take them to see her, Miss
Ossie Price, who had tended Prices' Store
six days a week for the lifetimes of both
generations, though the mother found it hard,
after she'd knocked on the door of the house
and Miss Ossie was standing there, so tired
and still not finished crying but polite
as always, to speak: "Ossie, I'm sorry
to ask this, but the children can't believe you
weren't in the fire. They never saw you
anywhere but in the store. Could you just
come out to the car and let them see you?"
The great burnt corpse that had been Prices' Store
lay just across the street, and it stung her
eyes even to glance that way, but she walked down
there and talked to them through the car window,
three little girls. The youngest, a tow-head,
a runny-nosed pretty one named Christine,
sat frozen and wide-eyed until Miss Ossie
opened the door, pulled the child into her
arms and hugged her close. Finally Christine
cried. Then they thanked Miss Ossie and drove home.

This was in Ivanhoe, Virginia,

a Blue Ridge Mountain town so small there's no

store there at all now that Prices' has burnt.

My mother, who lives there and who heard it

from somebody, told me this, but I've filled

in such details as I need to live with it,

as did my mother and her reliable

source, and as will those children, forgetting

it and holding on to it through the years

until one day that little one, who smelled

to Miss Ossie like a country child in need

of a bath, whose cheek left a smear of tears

and mucus on her dress, will be telling it

to her friend over lunch in some city

restaurant, the story will be spilling

out with such passion that they will both laugh,

and this well-dressed woman with a mountain

twang in her voice will find herself saying,

"This actually happened to me, I

remember it clearly," as in amazement

she asks herself, "Why am I making this up?"

Eastern Standard

Riled by Daylight
Savings, Grandmama
Huddle kept her
clocks unchanged.
Summers she was off
an hour and irked
at the Democrats
responsible
for inflation,
integration,
and now this
further indignity.

Disoriented
her last years
in a nursing home,
she shrank
until she became
an old-lady doll,
restrained in bed
and railing
to the bare,
urine-scented
room about bad food,
bad manners,
and the Kennedys.

At ninety-nine
she finally died.
I'm forty-seven.
Yesterday I stole
an hour
from a clock of hers
that has come down
to me. This morning
when I checked
my watch
against the light
outside the window,
my grandmother
spoke sharply:
"What time
is it, sonny?
And don't you
lie to me!"

Study

This morning rain on my skylight
marbles the blue-gray sky and blurs
the maple's branches suffering
the wind from the northeast.
                              A bird
flashes diagonally up
across the wet-streaked glass,
winged shadow there and gone so fast
I barely see it;
               then standing
at my grandmother's grave, I feel
my mother lean against me, wind
and cold rain slapping our faces
for letting Gran die by herself
in a hateful room;
                  and driving
through mountains in a slick-tired VW
with one headlight gone, I'm swabbing
fog off the windshield while rain turns
to snow;
        dark is coming, and I
am saying goodbye to Linda
Butler on Dundalk Avenue
in thin rain that's chilling us both,
shivering us hard these minutes
that are the last we ever spend
together;
         a boy on a porch
smells rain coming across the fields
and sees his young father running
toward him with drops splattering
his shirt;
          a child out in the yard
hears his aunt laugh as he strips off
clothes in a thunderstorm—
                         quick light
flashing down corridors darkened
by all these years!—
                   as a crow lights,
bobbing a limb of my neighbor's spruce,
or lifts and flies through fifty miles
of rain before it comes to rest.

The Nature of Yearning

for Lindsey and Bess

I

This Northern August swells with warmth

the garden would burst and a trout waits

beneath the moving river surface

he holds steady until the brown caddis

fly floats above him he plunges upward

breaks the silent water then slaps down fat

as deer that graze the flat meadows while slowly

as in a dream of shadows a black bear circles

beneath trees ten thousand shades of green.

II

All changed now quickened the morning

air in September lifts the spirit high

as one perfect trumpet note still

this clarity this concerto suggests

the coming death of tomato vines also

cucumber broccoli corn beans peas yellow

squash cauliflower all vegetables dead

or dying we wait the swelling of pumpkins

the blood flame turning of delicate leaves.

III

High down out of Canada the geese were flying

all day my wife said that far-off honking

sound makes you feel lonely the trees were pure

fire for two weeks but now the leaves have fallen

all purple and brown the woods resound with axes

while men cut logs the children home from school

go out for kindling the leaves crackle the blood

of the animals flows richer and a white-tail doe

sniffs the air at dusk her smoky fawn now half-grown.

IV

Chop the caught turkey's neck catch the buck

deer in gunsights fire shots deep into his heart

sling up his carcass to a thick tree cut open

his belly and handle the bloody heat and stink

of his guts shoot doves partridge quail

pheasant and grouse shoot rabbits shoot quick

squirrels and walk the stubbled fields with meat

on your back for soon the snow comes and with it

the silence at night when the wind wants man flesh.

V

White December the elegance of pine trees

in snow with voices rising in praise of Christ

the soft child of winter all Bach Fasch

and Handel cannot hold Jesus' swelling song

but now the trout takes no food the bass

sinks into the darkest pools of the river

the bear's blood slows while goose and duck

have long flown south and beside the house

snow deepens over logs stacked for the fire.

VI

Ice ice the death of trees the wind strips them bare

it whips them into savage rooted dances branches

crack limbs are yanked off they fall and smatter

on the frozen ground fearing wind I tell my wife

don't stand by that window a pane might burst

this morning she found stiff on the crusty ice

a redpoll dead and light as dust in her hand she said

the sun has forgotten us the nights go on and on

the clouds flee and the wind howls all day long.

VII

No meat in the house we cut holes in the ice

this February we fished for smelt and perch the ice

on the lake was two feet thick my wife thinks

the birds have left us forever only the rats thrive

they steal our corn and leave us just cobs and husks

rabbits are hard to track now but one the other day

sat in the field he was so cold I walked up and kicked

him before I shot the ice builds its kingdom

and holds against what fire we have left love.

VIII

We long for warmth these days there is little sun

still no birds have flown north over our house

and I think this March no month for birth only

the wind has life no green anywhere the trees

are just bones they shiver and bend they want

loose from this earth yesterday we saw the grass

it was brown and dead as an old hide in daylight

the snow melts some but it freezes again at night

the ground is covered with brittle crusts of thin ice.

IX

Oh the waters burst there are the timid green buds

delicate grass crocus and daffodil the waters

gather they flow out of the mountain the streams

wash off dead limbs and leaves the gentle rains

bring birth this air of April wakes even the animals

the spring birds have come back the trout leaps again

now the wind is a child the earth is sunlight a woman

walks outside this morning she is beautiful as the clear

sweet sound a man makes with his horn at his lips.

Visit of the Hawk

Across the blank blue of my study window
passed a wingspan of such consequence
that I stopped my work and sat still, certain
of something. I recall that the hairs
on the back of my neck were not standing on end.

Nevertheless:

I stood up, went straight to the skylight,
opened it and looked out, then peculiarly
knew to look back over the pitch of the roof
into the ragged green leaves and zig-zag twigs
of the butternut tree, where with savage aplomb

perched the hawk.

Urban Man Extends Head from Cockpit of House, Cranes
Neck and Observes Chicken Hawk in Butternut Tree
was the tableau, and a man with enough gumption
to have received the hawk's message that it had
come to that tree might have been expected to

understand

that the moment was purely and exclusively
just what it was, a moment, an invitation
to give over oneself to regarding the hawk.
But suddenly jittery, I began to doubt what
I plainly saw and ducked back inside to call

to my wife.

When she came upstairs, I felt this absurd relief.
Together we snuck to the skylight, poked our heads
into the airy world, and brushed against each other
most pleasantly, though of course what we saw was no
grandly feathered breast but merely a slightly

bobbing twig.

Inside the Hummingbird Aviary

Thumb-sized birds in gaudy greens,
iridescent vermilions, stop
on invisible floating dimes
intricately to pivot and kiss

sugar-water bottles or desert
blossoms. Within easy snatching
distance, a Broad-billed perches,
preens, pisses in a quick squirt,

darts out a tongue half
its body length. Suddenly
suspended at breast level,
a Calliope confronts a man,

marking its possession of that
quadrant of space, the sheer force
of its watch-part heart stopping
the giant, making him laugh.

These wings are the furious
energy of perfect stillness
to make him forget kestrels
and red-masked vultures.

Here in this airy cage
he has seen five whole
hummingbirds fit
into the chambers

of his hog-sized heart.
What the man wants now
is to be desert soil
beneath a thorny bush,

the black tongues of hummers
engineering sweetness
from blossoms that once
were his body.

Perspective

This morning finches come
to my window feeder.

Sunlight sifts through
the cedar by the garage

by which a black cat
crouches, waiting.

Together this cat and I
study the finches,

I from the sofa, seeing
in sequence, window, birds,

sunlight, tree, and cat,
and cat seeing, I suppose,

beneath a veil of cedar
needles, the feeding winged

creatures that quicken
its pulse. Long seconds

we hold still, absorbed
by what we see. Then

cat inches closer,
finches fly,

and I sit with my mind
leaping, claws extended,

but winging off with every
feather still intact.

The Feeder

A boy, I shot
a chickadee
so many times
that when it fell
it was more
a bag of BB's
than a bird.

Poachers shoot
mountain gorillas,
amputate their feet,
hands, and heads
for souvenirs,
catch their babies
and sell them.

This finch perched
at my window
is scarlet of back,
breast, and head,
its mate gray, streaked
with darker gray.
What is the weight
of two adult finches?
A few quarters
and some dimes?

Go away.
Holy creatures
of the planet,
please forsake us.

Feeder in the Dark

Square tube of molded plastic
surrounded by a steel grid
with steel top and bottom, it
hangs invisibly in the dark.

Designed to baffle squirrels,
the thing has the look
of a bomb, torpedo, torture
device, or tiny prison.

In these early morning hours
this small cage hangs outside
my window, just hangs there
in the dark, in the rain.

My black windows are changing
to blue. The first sparrow
flies to my feeder, clasps
its rungs, takes its seed.

Soon the unbaffled squirrels
will climb my window screen,
jump to the feeder, and hang
upside down to eat their fill.

The Snow Monkey Argues With God

Four days the mother
Snow Monkey carries
her still-born baby
before she leaves it

by a rocky stream. Then
she finds a high place
where she can brood alone
and still see her sisters

with their babies.
Four days she groomed
what should have been
as lively as these others.

If the Snow Monkey hurts
this way, can she not
also know what death is?
Or at least what it is not.

The thing she left downstream,
is not like these babies,
tugging and pulling
at their mothers, trying

to focus four-day-old
eyes on falling water
and sunlight skittering
under moving tree-branches.

While she watches her sisters
tenderly nursing
their young, she must feel
the wordless

old quarrel: better
that this paradise be burnt
to a clean white ash
than for any living

creature to have to lay down
on streamside rocks
what has been loved, what
stinks to high heaven.

Discovery Channel

>Beneath comedy
>are mating
>Arctic foxes:
>
>the female
>groveling,
>snappish,
>
>the male so quick
>to mount, humping
>mechanically,
>
>and his face
>stretched, idiotic,
>blank. Then he's done.
>
>Only briefly is
>she in heat. Quickly
>they perform again.

In my rural seventh grade class was a big boy named James
Bledsoe, older than all of us, held back two or three years,
This James Bledsoe characteristically took his pleasure from
turning around in his seat to set a sheet of lined notepaper
on Faye Sutphin's desk, drawing a circle with a dot in the
middle of it and asking Faye if that was what her titty
looked like, drawing another with some curlicues around it
and asking Faye... Mrs. Jackson wouldn't confront James
unless she had to, and Faye wasn't a nice enough girl to get
by with telling on James, but then she also wasn't a bad
or a big enough girl to kick James in the nuts and make him
stop. It went on for months that way, James getting our
attention when he did it, Faye blushing and sweating and
grinning and blinking back tears.

>Seeing animals
>sets me to thinking
>about God.
>
>I know this is just
>my Protestant
>upbringing.
>
>Seeing mating
>Arctic foxes
>brings to mind
>
>what James showed us
>when he leaned close
>to Faye's bowed head,
>
>a profoundly
>brutal intelligence
>at work.

Party Poem

It is only when you watch the dense mass of thousands of ants, crowded together, blackening the ground, that you begin to see the whole beast, and now you can observe it thinking, planning, calculating. It is an intelligence, a kind of live computer, with crawling bits for its wits.
        Lewis Thomas
        The Lives of a Cell

This woman I knew slightly
both of us with a buzz
on at a cocktail party—
told me, "You know, David,"
and I guessed I probably
did, "there's this secret
everybody knows and nobody
ever tells..." I nodded
because I had always opined
exactly that, though what
this secret was I'd never
found words for. This was
a loud party, out on a green
lawn, everybody dressed up
in summer frocks and suits,
afternoon sunlight, glassy
high clouds, and I can tell
you, it was a day of grand
possibility, a proper day
for passing on the shocking
truth. "Men and women,"
she said, narrowing her eyes,
making a small sweep with her
drink in the air between us,
"no matter who they are or how
long they've been together..."
My acquaintance stepped forward
significantly as she trailed off,
paused with a hum of voices all
around us, and asked, "Do you
know what I mean?" and I told her
yes, though I wasn't sure.
Couples everywhere we looked
among these party-goers, new
ones talked with each other,

old ones talked separately
with somebody else, and some
were half of an old and half
of a new, and the ones that
weren't half of any couple
looked like they would be
soon. My friend and I had
spouses and children at home,
and our interest in each other
was slight. I looked away
toward the trees and wondered
exactly what she and I were
up to with our talk. I saw
that on my friend's forehead
were these tiny beads of sweat
just where her dark hair swept
back to a silver barrette,
and catching the slightest
whiff of her scented bathsoap,
I lifted my clear plastic cup
to hers—we were both down
to a puny cube or two and some
dead twists of lime. We clinked
these dreadful cups together
and chimed, "To the secret!"
We drained what we had left,
then without saying a word,
turned and ambled through
the crowd toward the bar.
Minutes later this Cathy and I
let ourselves be caught up
in conversation with other
friends, let ourselves be forever
separated (though of course
at the party we didn't think
of it that way). Well, maybe
we did exchange a postcard or two
before we finally let it stand
that time was going to have
its way with us. Now her last
name comes to me only if I
concentrate, and I doubt she even
remembers how easily we moved
together across the grass or how
at the same moment I lifted
my elbow toward her she raised
her hand lightly to take my arm.

American History

Young, they meet and tell each other
everything, exchanging childhoods,
as members of different tribes
present gifts at their first meeting
to signal their desire for peace.

The boy grew up with hog-killing,
had a knife-fight in high school,
jumped from airplanes in Germany,
and interrogated farmers
who denied they were Viet Cong.

The girl knew about monsoon heat.
In college she'd gone to India
for a month and stopped being the girl
who spent summers at the club, swimming
and playing tennis with her sister.

Talking this way, he sees her life
as what he was raised to want.
She sees his as the struggle
she's been denied. Her tenderness
comes freely; he wills his into shape.

Years later, when they are raising
children, the woman can't always
remember not to tease the man
with a kitchen knife in her hand,
and the man still hasn't learned

how to chat politely at parties.
But they don't mind remembering how
when they first met, he couldn't hear enough
about her birthday sleepovers,
nor she about his fucked-up army pals.

The Swimmer

With her husband rowing
a boat beside her,

a woman is swimming across
a lake five miles wide.

She can do it. Daily
she swims fifty laps

in the pool at the Y;
nevertheless, here is

her husband in case
anything goes wrong

on such a windless
mid-summer day.

He's never been
a swimmer, but now

this sweating husband's
sweeping strokes become

so rhythmical that he
begins to dream of diving

into the cool lake,
his delighted wife

following him, the two
of them swimming down to a point

above a vast underwater
configuration of plants,

rocks, sand, and circling
schools of colored fish.

He sees a pale man and woman
coolly suspended, gazing

down through the blue water
toward a huge snapping turtle

that slowly glides beneath them.
Meanwhile the steadily swimming

wife begins to envision her own
magical rising from the water,

her body's strokes powering
her up into the air

above her amazed husband,
who now witnesses how one

kick of her leg earns her five
feet of altitude, one

rotation of her arm
propels her through ten

feet of air, so that he
laughs and praises her

while rowing furiously
trying not to lose sight

of her. But already she
is learning to swerve,

dart, and dive above him,
soar straight up until

he becomes tiny. How easily
she floats down and settles

beside him! All this while,
the two of them continue

their tedious progress,
the husband keeping

his little boat a sensible
distance away from the wife

whose strokes and breathing
he monitors occasionally,

now and then glancing
at his watch, now and then

catching (as if she were
a whale or a porpoise)

his wife's eye that fastens
on him half a moment

when her face rolls up out
of the water, his wife's eye

that locks in focus
on his face that split

second before closing
as she rolls her face

back down beneath
the water's skin.

The Quick

His wife's thumbnail,
bitten short that way
tells the man nothing,
though he finds himself
oddly aware of it.
He has never seen her
put her teeth to it.

So one day he asks her,
When you do this,
what do you think about?
Lightly he touches her thumb.
Nothing, she says.
Color comes to her face.
She puts that hand in her lap
and covers it with the other.

Upstairs that night he finds her
sitting on the edge of their bed
in the dark, in only her slip,
her arms crossed, her head bowed.
When he kneels in front of her,
and reaches to take down
the little straps, he knows
what she is about to say:
Don't. Please don't.

Quiet Hour

Sometimes after dinner
they dawdle long after

the kids have excused
themselves. Then their

talk pleases them, what
her boss told her today,

a small thing he repaired,
something a teacher said

to their oldest. Tonight
it would be easy to ask,

When should we separate?
Who'll stay in the house?

How are we going to share
the children? She could

say, Do you know how hard
it's been living with you

all these years hating you
so much? He could tell her

he's thought of leaving
every day. From the air

they could pluck these words,
then maybe the forgiving ones

would come, too, I know
I haven't been, you did

the best you, and we tried,
we really, or maybe what came

would be the deeply bitter
you son of a, you goddamn.

So the words they choose
for these last moments

of sputtering candlelight
hold the weight of their

separate lifetimes, what
futures their children may

expect, and finally whether
death will be cruel or kind

to them: *I guess I'd
better do these dishes. No,*

*you're tired, I'll do them,
you just stay put.*

Music

Last night his clumsy love
for her was Dvorak's
noble Cello Concerto.
Today her sadness
over the ways he has
failed her became
Roberta Flack's
elegant mourning
of her baby who's
never coming back.
Their vague feelings
go on drifting
through the house
for years until one day
he switches on the radio
and accidentally plays
the last eight bars
of something—Song
of the Domestic Broadsword,
Song of the Dead Children,
Song of Twelve Billion Light
Years of Frozen Space. Then
the man will almost turn
over his chair, hurrying
to retrieve the silence.
The woman will go on
sitting there, wincing,
with the magazine open
on her lap. But of course
they can't unplay a song
like that, a song in which
they heard how they can't
bear even one more day
together.

The Birds

Driving a dirt road, a man
and his wife see flashes
of a yellow like a new crayon,

then a blue so brightly
royal that the husband stops
as if the bird were a traffic light.

Actually there are three
birds, this otherworldly
blue one, perched on a roadside

bramble so close to their car
they can see its tufted head
and orange beak, then a little

further away the yellow
with black-barred wings,
and down in the road gravel

like some scruffy cousin,
a plain sparrow, a bird
of so little distinction

they ignore it altogether.
Years after their divorce,
the husband remembers

that afternoon and what
a gift they took the birds
to be—his wife talked

so happily about how
long she could still see
the blue and the yellow

in their dipping flight
away down the slope of green
hillside toward a wall

of sumac. They spoke only
of the blue and the yellow,
and he wonders now what happened

to the third, the greyish-brown
that he doesn't recall
seeing take flight.

Summer Lake

The slow coming of dusk over the water

enthralls the husband and wife.

What soft shades of light the lake

and the sky turn, such dark lavenders

and pinks they must believe their wish

to be happy together has produced this

world around them.

                    Here on the rocky

beach at the back of the park

an old man playing an accordian

turns toward them, cocks his head,

and launches a serenade. A blue van

he has apparently driven here

holds a woman and some children

who sit inside it, unmoving, staring

out over the water.

                    The aching husband

puts his arm around his soul-tired

wife's shoulders, she puts hers

around his waist, and they stand like that

on the grassy slope above the beach

listening,

          because the old musician

seems accomplished, squeezing and pulling

a stream of notes from the instrument,

rippling his fingers up and down

its buttons and keys, smiling at them

as he plays.

    "He's brilliant, or else

he's terrible," the wife murmurs

in that way they've come to speak, out

toward some disinterested witness,

but her husband is in a mood to take it

intimately and so nods and says, "Yes,

I've never heard anything like that. Maybe

it's wonderful."

    But they don't know

what to make of the music, though they try

to listen even harder. The notes sound

crushed together, too many and too strange.

"I don't like it," the wife finally says,

abruptly turning away and walking across the grass

with her head down.

    Silky light

gilds the water, the accordian man grins,

and the park's spring green burns

his eyes, so that the husband must turn

away, too. Stumbling now, he almost runs

to catch up with his wife in her pale dress

steadily moving into the shadows

of houses, trees, gardens and lawns.

                        Later,

riding the ferry across the lake, he

and she stand at the rear of the boat,

gazing back across the wake's churned-up

froth and long ripples of inky blue water

toward the lakeside park, where now

there is no battered blue van, nothing

but a light rim of beach stones beneath

the deep green of grass and trees almost

in darkness.

              Why they stand back here,

instead of forward with the other passengers

taking the wind in their faces and smiling

toward the lighted city is not something

these two wish to discuss. But they know this

is what they want: to study the receding

shore haloed by dull pink light, stand

together without touching, and go on

hearing what the little man played for them.

Asylum

He has seduced the daughter
of a high school girlfriend
and this mother is so furious
that she has written to tell . . .

To whom she has written
he doesn't know, but he wakes

feeling awful, feeling certain
he has ruined the girl's life
and his own, but then understanding
that this has been merely a dream,

he begins testing it for truth.
Judy Richardson was his girlfriend.

He's seen her maybe five times
in thirty years, but he knows
she has daughters. In his mind
there is the image of a young girl

anyone would have loved, a lively,
funny girl with an intelligent face

and slender arms that he's afraid
might have held him, a girl
like Judy, for whom he deeply cared
years ago and who still makes him

smile when he remembers slow
dancing with her. But as he thinks

of this daughter, he knows there was
between them that kind of sex
from which no one ever recovers,
and he knows he committed harm

to this good girl whom he meant
only to love. He tries to see

her completely, but her shoulder,
her neck, half her torso fade away.
He tells himself it was a dream,
there was no girl like that.

He tells himself he is free
of that crime, his life is

his own again, it is sunny out,
he must make coffee, pour juice,
toast bread and butter it. But ugly
pieces of the girl float through

his vision as he showers, as if he
has dismembered her and the terrible

parts of her wait for him downstairs.
Just a dream, he chants against
the face facing him as he shaves.
Just a dream, he says aloud,

shivering as he dresses. At last
he stands and slips over his head

his old blue sweater, cotton, washed
a dozen times, limp, familiar as rain
spattering his windowpane, and in that
instant he thinks he is all right.

Creation Myth

Suddenly sharply awake,
the man is intensely aware
of floating on azure water.

Like an image arisen
in some planet-sized brain,
from the pitch of deep sleep

he has appeared in sunlight
in a small white sailboat anchored
in jewel-green water above

a sea-floor of rippled sand.
What happiness this man feels,
gazing downward: the water

is ecstasy. The man lets
his hand and fingers paddle
through it, lets his pale wrist sink

and rise. Suddenly he knows
a woman is here with him,
she is near enough to touch,

and perhaps she is happy, too,
though he cannot see her face,
cannot seem to turn toward her.

Why, then, does he imagine her
wearing his blue shirt, eyes closed,
smiling upward, her brow damp,

her legs brown and glistening?
Why can't he turn and the two
of them start moving their little

white boat toward the island
the man now knows lies just off
to the west? How long does he mean

to keep splashing in sea water?
Any moment her concentration
may falter. Even now, coasting

at terrific speed
across the ocean floor
toward that blip

on the water's surface,
comes the shadow of something
relentless and starving.

A Field in North Dakota

The man imagines a field of trees.

The field is in North Dakota where he has never been.

The trees are hemlocks.

It is daylight, early spring.

There are animals and birds, clouds, small plants, rocks,

but it is the trees that interest him.

They are widely spaced.

Near the ground their branches are thick and slanted outward.

Toward the top the branches become smaller,

angled upward to the sunlight.

The trunks of these trees are huge and straight.

They are rooted into the ground in thick knots and gnarls.

The trunks give with the wind and sometimes creak.

Of course the trees are green, the old needles a darker shade,

the new growth a fresh lighter green.

The trunks and branches are covered with a brown shaley bark.

The sappy wood inside is a light honey color, streaked with red.

These hemlocks are surrounded by the smell of hemlock,

and many needles have fallen to the earth beneath them.

These have turned a bright rust color.

Tired of the daylight and the pleasant season,

the man imagines the hemlocks at night, deep in winter.

They loom in the moonlight, weighted with snow.

He lets the wind from Canada howl down among them,

shaking their branches free of the heavy clumps.

The landscape pleases him,

and so he places a girl in the snow field

and lets her dance among the hemlocks, her dark hair flying.

Now it is the girl who interests him.

Of course she is cold,

but he prefers that she go on dancing from hemlock to hemlock.

Eventually the wind will kill her,

but for now she is happy in her quick movement in the moonlight.

She loves how the snow sparkles,

how the trees creak, how the branches sway.

Her fingers are numb, but she moves them anyway

in graceful gestures of which she has no knowledge.

She is absorbed in the larger movements

of her arms, her knees, her thighs, her bruised feet.

When she falls, her hair lies flown across the snow

where the wind swirls it constantly.

Beneath the girl there are layers of snow and crusted ice,

and beneath that a frozen mat of grass,

then dirt and stones, then solid rock

going deep down to the earth's core.

Above the girl there is the night, the wind, the moon,

a few clouds, several million stars, endless space.

This girl speaks only French and mostly talks about dancing.

The man's language is American, his feet are clumsy,

and he spends his time sitting down in warm rooms.

The wind goes on moving through the hemlocks.

Toward dawn it will begin to snow again.

He strains to hear each frail heartbeat.

The Dance

The child learns to dance
alone
in a room with music.
Her body
doesn't know
what to do, but it wants
to do something.
She moves one foot,
then another.

Newly in love, a girl and a boy
hear a song they like.
They try moving
with each other and laugh
at how clumsy they are.
Ah, but they learn it all
so quickly.

Consider the man and the woman.
Say, it's New Year's Eve,
say, they go to a party,
and somebody plays that song
they learned to dance to
and while dancing learned
they wanted to marry each other.
Of course they don't sit there!
They move so smoothly
their bodies'
intelligence
fills the whole room.

We know all this.
One leaves
or one dies
or one is conveyed
to the Home of Guaranteed Prolonged Misery,
and the other is left
alone
in a room where music
is possible even if she is
just sitting there
remembering some
old song that makes
her body
sway.

Love and Art

At the Chagall Exhibit
the woman moves slowly
from picture to picture.

The man hardly pauses.
He eats the pictures,
wishing he could have
them all for himself.

Bella with a White Collar
surrounds the woman, as God
must cradle the universe.

The man strides past The Wedding,
Bride and Groom of the Eiffel Tower,
all of Daphnis and Chloe.
He is eager to buy postcards.

At the Magic Flute costumes,
the woman suddenly hears Chagall
and Mozart telling jokes, filling
the museum with their laughter.

The man buys a Fall of Icarus
T-shirt and a Milking the Cow poster
for the kids and sits down to wait.

Bella Writing is where she stops,
knowing the moment the painter
found her like that and took up
what was handy, a page of notepaper,

and that is where he finds her,
standing with strangers, brushing
her eyes, and smiling into the light.

Upstairs Hallway, 5 A.M.

My daughter's voice
wafts into the dark
through which, freshly
showered and shaved,
I am feeling my way.
I stop and listen
but hear only the house
hum, click, and groan.

A friend says a voice
on the phone instantly
reveals sex, age, ethnic
background, education
and intelligence.

But from this sentence
spoken out of her
dreams by my child,
I discern no words,
only a tone: quiet,
serious, friendly,
somewhat formal.

The dead must hear
their living speak
just this way: *Yes,
you are there forever
running your fingers
along the cool wall
of darkness, while I
so deeply dream this
world of sunlit shapes.
Soon enough I shall be
moving behind you.
Please, let me sleep
a little longer.*

Close

for Ted Littwin and
Lyn Mattoon

My friend tells me how,
in his childhood, his father
rose early, then got lonely
and so came to stand
over my friend's bed.

My friend says he would wake
from a deep sleep, aware
of his father's presence,
would sit straight up in bed
and say, "What are you doing in here?"

"Oh nothing," his father
would reply. "I wasn't bothering
anything, but now that you're up..."
and then they would be talking
all through those impossible hours.

Later, drinking and talking,
my friend and I consider the coming
death of the planet. "It's no longer
a matter of pushing a button
we don't want to push," I say.

He says, "Yes, all we have to do
is live exactly as we're living
right now." And I murmur,
"What do you think we have,
maybe a hundred years?"

Nodding with understanding how
we mean to murder our children,
he and I pierce our loneliness.
My own father is dead and anyway never
stood by my bed in the dark.

Another Father's Story

Already today too many
fathers have behaved badly.

One with his shabby shoes
embarrassed his daughters,

another simply left the house,
another still rages in the dreams

of his sons. I will never
forget the cardiologist

who so beautifully organized
his family's day at the beach,

then suddenly had to be stopped
from holding his daughter under.

"I'm sorry," he said,
"but she splashed me."

The grown children telling
these stories flinch from them,

as if their fathers go on surprising
them with their nasty antics,

as if they wished someone
would say, "No, that can't be true,

that's just not the way fathers
behave." I can say my father

gave his life to serving his family,
was never violent, and often loved

us heroically. I can say my friend
Tommy's dad, Buck Ingo, primitive-

looking, and filthy and stinking
from his work, gave Tommy goodnight

kisses of such tenderness
when I stayed with the Ingos

I almost asked him to kiss me, too.
I can say almost every day

my teenaged daughter angers me,
and I do not strike her.

But now there is this father,
who for years has forced himself

on his daughter, still trying
to frighten her out of giving

testimony, this huge, bearded
father with a belly big

as the hood of a Volkswagen,
glaring at his child as she tells

the unspeakable details of what
he has done to her. This one shifts

in his chair. He clears his throat
to speak: "I am sorry," he begins.

Catch

Barehanded, my father
caught my first throws.

Later I saw him
wincing but thought

his pain small
compared to my need

for dignity
at recess.

When he thought
I was old enough,

he began to fire
fast balls that stung

my fingers, that one
May dusk made me

cry and walk
into the house.

Ashamed in my room,
I heard him explain

what was wrong
to Mother downstairs.

Now when Molly asks
me to play catch

and she's got our
house's one glove,

my father softly
sighs, *All right, son.*

In my bare palm
I feel him

feeling what
I thought

I had
to give him.

Thinking About My Father

I have to go back
past the way he was
at the end, panting
for breath, begging
for medicine, crazy
from medicine taken
for years. This is
hard because in his
dying, he was vivid,
excruciatingly slow,
and profoundly self-
absorbed, as if his
death required more
energy and devotion
than we could ever
bring to his bedside.

But then there he is
at home, at his desk
in the den, where he
was able to be most
truly himself, paying
bills—he was happy
doing that—reading
the paper, then best
of all, beautifully
solving its crossword
puzzle. My father was
the absolute master
of crossword puzzles
in the *Roanoke Times*.

I do not mean to say
that he shut himself
off from us. It was
just that we learned
to approach his desk
for quiet attention.
He breathed a light
whistle between his
teeth while he helped
me balance my paper

route money, coat my
model airplane's silk
wing with banana oil,
hinge a new Brazilian
stamp into my album.

My father did things
with a care that was
more important to him
than the thing itself.
For example, painting
by the numbers: no one
ever number-painted so
gravely and precisely.
His Saint Bernards hang
over his desk, his blue
jays over the toilet so
that every peeing male
must witness the craft
of his terrible picture.

His pleasures were fresh
things, mail just pulled
from his post office box,
unthumbed newspapers, new
model airplane kits, sets
of mint-condition stamps
in glassine envelopes.
With his hands he savored
a new harmonica so that I
still see as sacred those
little Hohner boxes with
pictures on them of old-
time German concert bands.

I don't have any fresh
insight into my father
or his life. Thinking
about him like this, I
miss him, and I forget
how horrible his death
was. Some mornings I
wake up feeling bad for
no reason I can think of,
and then all day he'll be
on my mind, dying again.

I have no memory of his
holding me as an infant,
but we have an old home
movie in which my twenty-
two-year-old mother walks
out onto the front porch
and hands a baby to this
thin young man. Some days
I wake up limp and happy
as that child, smiled at
and lifted up to the sun
by someone who wanted me
right here in this world.

ACKNOWLEDGMENTS

The American Poetry Review: "Visit of the Hawk" and "Close"

Antioch Review: "Love and Art"

Boulevard: "The Swimmer"

The Journal: "Quiet Hour," "Creation Myth," and "Upstairs Hallway, 5 A.M."

The Kenyon Review: "The Birds" and "Thinking About My Father"

New Virginia Review: "The Snow Monkey Argues with God," "Study," and "Summer Lake"

Poetry: "Asylum"

Southern Poetry Review: "A Field in North Dakota"

The Sow's Ear: "Party Poem"

Texas Quarterly: "The Nature of Yearning"

Kentucky Poetry Review: "Catch"

The Gettysburg Review: "At the Desert Museum" and "Local Metaphysics"

The Old Red Kimono: "Another Father's Story" and "The Quick"

Colorado North Review: "Discovery Channel"

ABOUT THE AUTHOR

David Huddle lives in Burlington, Vermont. He teaches at the University of Vermont and at the Bread Loaf School of English.

THE PEREGRINE SMITH POETRY SERIES

Christopher Merrill, General Editor

Sequences, by Leslie Norris
Stopping by Home, by David Huddle
Daylight Savings, by Steven Bauer
The Ripening Light, by Lucile Adler
Chimera, by Carol Frost
Speaking in Tongues, by Maurya Simon
The Rebel's Silhouette, by Faiz Ahmed Faiz
    (translated by Agha Shahid Ali)
The Arrangement of Space, by Martha Collins
The Nature of Yearning, by David Huddle